THIS IS ME! 2022

THE WONDER OF WORDS

Edited By Iain McQueen

First published in Great Britain in 2022 by:

Young Writers
Remus House
Coltsfoot Drive
Peterborough
PE2 9BF
Telephone: 01733 890066
Website: www.youngwriters.co.uk

All Rights Reserved
Book Design by Ashley Janson
© Copyright Contributors 2022
Softback ISBN 978-1-80459-052-2

Printed and bound in the UK by BookPrintingUK
Website: www.bookprintinguk.com
YB0509V

FOREWORD

For Young Writers' latest competition This Is Me, we asked primary school pupils to look inside themselves, to think about what makes them unique, and then write a poem about it! They rose to the challenge magnificently and the result is this fantastic collection of poems in a variety of poetic styles.

Here at Young Writers our aim is to encourage creativity in children and to inspire a love of the written word, so it's great to get such an amazing response, with some absolutely fantastic poems. It's important for children to focus on and celebrate themselves and this competition allowed them to write freely and honestly, celebrating what makes them great, expressing their hopes and fears, or simply writing about their favourite things. This Is Me gave them the power of words. The result is a collection of inspirational and moving poems that also showcase their creativity and writing ability.

I'd like to congratulate all the young poets in this anthology, I hope this inspires them to continue with their creative writing.

CONTENTS

Bersted Green Primary School, Bognor Regis

Daisy Truelove (10)	1

Bowness Primary School, Little Lever

Kaycee	3
Aaryan	4
Alara Stoyanova (10)	5
Ben	6
Andy Herrera (10)	7
Lauren Rozsas (10)	8

Brooke CE (VC) Primary School, Brooke

Thomas Greenway (8)	9
Ted Albert-Worman (8)	10
Phoebe Carlson-Hoare (7)	11
Huxley Wolfe (7)	12
Millie Russell (8)	13
Olivia Higgins (7)	14
Toby A (8)	15
Tabitha Mather (7)	16
Ivy Long (7)	17
Eleanor Dzandza (7)	18
Jonty (7)	19
Toby Bellwood (7)	20
George Bircham (8)	21
Cecily (7)	22
Katie Bellwood (7)	23
Imogen Wright (7)	24
Kieran Warman (7)	25
Zoey Holleman (8)	26
Toby Swietlik (8)	27
Jake (7)	28
Felix Mott (7)	29
Audrey Fairhurst (7)	30
Sergio Howard (7)	31
Harry Ashmole (7)	32
Isaac (8)	33

Falconbrook Primary School, Battersea

Israh Azgaou (8)	34
Asma Nishat (8)	35
Iman Asif (8)	36
Archie Martin (8)	37

Montgomery Primary Academy, Sparkbrook

Zara Holden (9)	38
Zara Naz Asif (9)	39
Maria Jamil (9)	40
Issa Abdulnahed (8)	41

Moor Park Primary School, Bispham

Karolina Malon (9)	42
Louisa Lee (9)	43
Sienna May Bampton (9)	44
Alfie Jai (9)	45
Esmee Pogson (10)	46
Milo Clarke (10)	47
Lily Sue (9)	48
Mia Carmen (10)	49
Lacie-Mae (9)	50

Our Lady Queen Of Peace Catholic Engineering College, Skelmersdale

Lucy Johnson (11)   51

Pilling St John's CE School, Pilling

Tamara Al Jammal (9)	52
Aurora Wrigley (9)	53
Joseph Goth (11)	54
Amelia Jayne Ratcliffe (7)	55
Elsie Ellis (9)	56
Maiyah Newbould (8)	57
Eliza Clitheroe (8)	58
Ruby Sarson (10)	59

Preston Tower Primary School, Prestonpans

Harry Burgoyne (9)	60
Ashley Tait (9)	61
Dylan Gare (9)	62
Josh Quinn (9)	63
Aaron Trendell (9)	64
Lois Buchannan (9)	65
Ava Gray (9)	66
Skye Mcewan (9)	67
Olivia Linda Thorburn	68
Kayla Reid (9)	69
Harry Davidson (10)	70
Lucy Betts (9)	71
Riley Harrison (9)	72
Callum Stewart (9)	73
Ava Rawlison (9)	74
Alex Kubis-Simpson (9)	75
Sophie Dickson (9)	76
Georgie Ritchie (9)	77
Sophie Scott (9)	78
Lucy Spence (9)	79
Logan Brand (9)	80
Emillie Clark (9)	81
Harry Fitzpatrick (9)	82
Ollie Gray (9)	83

Jessica Skinner (9)	84
Freddie Young	85

Sacred Heart RC Primary School, Blackburn

Muskaan Ahmed (9)   86

Sherington Primary School, London

Ipsit Jagtap (7)   88

South Rise Primary School, London

Glory Ano Sunday (10)	89
Krista Thapa (9)	90
Rebecca Roper (10)	92
Desireoluwa Oduneye (10)	93

Spen Valley Sports College, Liversedge

Maisie Wilkinson (13)	94
Leah Womersley (11)	95
Miah Taylor (11)	96

Springhallow School, Ealing

Sarim Khan (10)	97
Kj Johnson (10)	98

St John Fisher Primary School, Littlemore

Seyi Fowowe (10)	99
Tyreign Thomas (10)	100

Westlea Primary School, Westlea

Emily Mcmahon (9)	101
Yusuf Karakaya (11)	102
Otter Ley (10)	104
Emily M (10)	106
Iris Hinder (9)	107

Jaxon Coe (9)	108
Oliver Libby (9)	109
Thea Smolarek (9)	110
Rizwaan (11)	111
Toby Sieluzycki (9)	112
Leo Hedges (10)	113
Bailey Mussard (10)	114
Samantha Belina	115
Jessica (11)	116
Jenson Cain (10)	117
Isabelle Le Leivre (10)	118
Amelia Cheesley (10)	119
Ellie Mortimer (11)	120
Cole Farley (9)	121
Aislinn Thompson (11)	122
Nikola Kozlowska (10)	123
Janelle (10)	124
Jackson Bridgman (9)	125
Ollie Wallis (11)	126
Isabelle Fraser (11)	127
Josh Saji (10)	128
Kieran Butler (10)	129
Izzy Harper (10)	130
Jermain Dube (10)	131
Imogen Green (10)	132
Sayam (10)	133
James Bell (10)	134
Emily Pentecost (10)	135
Ruby Burns (10)	136
Sebastian Piechowicz (9)	137
Max Bunney (10)	138
Arish Siddique (10)	139
Morgan Salmon (9)	140
Leo Jones (10)	141
Eliza Etmanska (10)	142
Maisie Bowles (10)	143
Maysie Cope (10)	144
Alfie Lusty (11)	145
Callum Shurey (10)	146
Billii-Mae Hemmings-Willott (11)	147
Rhys Huff (10)	148
Archie Walsh (10)	149
Ianis Butnariu (10)	150
Jamie Lea (10)	151

Wood Lane Primary School, Bignall End

Noah D (11)	152

THE POEMS

This Is Me

Hello there, my name is Daisy
I'm ten years old and very crazy
I go to a football club, it's really fun
I love to play it under the sun
I love theatre and drama
My favourite animal is a koala
My favourite colour is blue
I like purple too
I have a little sister called Rosie
She can be a little nosey
Her passion is gymnastics
She really is fantastic
Let me tell you about my mummy
Her food is rather yummy
She works as an air hostess
She looks really fancy in her dress
She loves to fly to exotic places
But she always says we're her favourite faces
That was a little bit about me and mine

Hope I see you again sometime
I hope you enjoyed all that's above
That's it, from Daisy Truelove.

Daisy Truelove (10)
Bersted Green Primary School, Bognor Regis

This Is Me

Tantalising and tall
I'm not very good at football
English isn't really my thing
But art and history to me are like a diamond ring

I love to chill and play games at home
Sometimes I love being alone
I adore my computer
When I win, I feel super

School is one of my prime concerns
Sometimes it gets on my nerves
Occasionally my work is like a brand new car
Occasionally my work is a bit bizarre

So this is me
Sometimes bluey, sometimes smiling with glee
And to bring things to a speedy end
I'm quite easy to befriend.

Kaycee
Bowness Primary School, Little Lever

This Is Me

Talkative, chatty
Sometimes I go very batty
My mind is overly crowded
Sometimes my thoughts are enshrouded

CG5 is my man
I'm just his biggest fan
He's made so many songs
He just deserves the applause

In comes Badboy Halo
He is someone you may know
He's going down the music path
But now has to feel Smeppy's wrath

Muffin is their very best song
It will be with me all life long

I am the god of raps
And that is all of the facts
So see you later
You alligator.

Aaryan
Bowness Primary School, Little Lever

This Is Me

Zippy, crazy
I'm hardly Mrs Daisy
But maths is my power
But English makes me cower

I jump, I run
I like to have lots of fun
A lifelong basketball fan
I'm a crazy sort of lady
With a quirky sense of fashion

I'm sweet, I'm sour
Depending on the hour
Sometimes I'm loud
But of that I'm proud

Most days I'm moody
But some days are good

So this is me
Sometimes crazy, hardly Mrs Daisy.

Alara Stoyanova (10)
Bowness Primary School, Little Lever

This Is Me

I'm brilliant, I'm wise,
I reach the highest skies.
I adore writing code,
At school or my abode.

I can swim like a shark,
At every waterpark.
I'll race you in a pool,
Make you look like a fool.

I love to game,
And earn some fame.
At PVP, I'm a god,
I like to play Gary's Mod.

So this is me,
Never sad, always happy.
And to bring bad moods to a quick end,
I rely on my fantastic group of cray friends.

Ben
Bowness Primary School, Little Lever

This Is Me

A very smart mind
Also really kind
I like to do sports
Of each and every sort

Building I adore
I never get bored
I'm planning to build
As I am deeply skilled

Drumming I can do
It'll impress you
I enjoy to bake
But I make mistakes

Dodgeball is epic
I am athletic
Catching, I'm in charge
Dodging, I'm the sarge

So this is me
I am free
I am who I'm meant to be.

Andy Herrera (10)
Bowness Primary School, Little Lever

This Is Me

Kind, caring
I'm always sharing
Calling friends is what I do
Playing Roblox through and through

I play, I play
On sunny days
A lifelong watermelon fan
I eat them when I can

I'm kind, I'm sweet
Playing with my friends makes me feel complete
I'm sometimes shy.

Lauren Rozsas (10)
Bowness Primary School, Little Lever

Thomas

T errific Thomas is friendly and happy
H ealthy, outdoorsy Thomas, always ready to help
O thers in distress say I'm brave, sporty, quick and ready to help
M agnificent Thomas likes dressing up
A mazing Thomas is kind and caring
S trong at rugby - record six tries! I am Thomas, your friend, your hero!

Thomas Greenway (8)
Brooke CE (VC) Primary School, Brooke

Edward

E dward or people call me Ted
D ens, I love days out too
W alking in nature and climbing trees
A ll books I love, especially these, Dragon Training, Hogwarts too
R ugby, cricket, tennis too, but all sports mean stuff to me
D avid Attenborough is my hero, an awesome adventurer like I want to be.

Ted Albert-Worman (8)
Brooke CE (VC) Primary School, Brooke

Phoebe

P ractising singing in my room
H oping to go swimming soon
O oo, that's what I say when I see mint choc chip ice cream
E xcited to do the make-up of my dreams
B eing kind, respectful and safe, that's my thing
E mma Watson, she's my favourite actor, but Daniel Radcliffe is the king.

Phoebe Carlson-Hoare (7)
Brooke CE (VC) Primary School, Brooke

Huxley

H ealthy and helpful Huxley
U nderstanding and a good friend
X box is my favourite thing to play, FIFA 22 is where I will stay
L ooking forward to playing football with my team next Thursday
E xcited to score another goal
Y ou will hear the crowd as they lose control.

Huxley Wolfe (7)
Brooke CE (VC) Primary School, Brooke

Millie

M usic is my favourite
I have a puppy, his name is Barney
L ove to dance and party
L ittle me as small as a mouse
I like to do cheerleading
E vents are my favourite, don't get me started with the cakes
R espectful and safe is my thing.

Millie Russell (8)
Brooke CE (VC) Primary School, Brooke

Olivia

O n travel, I am very sick
L ovely and incredible that is me
I love dogs, especially when they splash in the sea
V ery nice and cuddly
I like ice cream, my favourite is mint
A ctive and energetic, when I'm running, I like to sprint.

Olivia Higgins (7)
Brooke CE (VC) Primary School, Brooke

Toby A

T alented at cricket and football.
O bjects float around me like cricket balls.
B asketballs are fun to play with.
Y ou will find me on the cricket pitch all day.

A nts get hurt when I am bowling the ball on the ground.

Toby A (8)
Brooke CE (VC) Primary School, Brooke

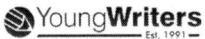

Tabitha

T abitha likes to play every day
A lways kind, happy and fun
B eing kind and nice
I like baking and camping
T abitha likes to brush her teeth
H appy all the time
A pples are my favourite food.

Tabitha Mather (7)
Brooke CE (VC) Primary School, Brooke

Ivy

I vy is important and intelligent
V ery polite and kind
Y ou can always help me

L oving listening and learning
O tters are cheeky
N ice and respectful
G lamorous and sometimes grumpy.

Ivy Long (7)
Brooke CE (VC) Primary School, Brooke

Eleanor

E leanor is intelligent
L oves dancing and gymnastics
E ncanto is my favourite film
A pples are my favourite fruit
N uku is my brother
O tters are kind
R eady, respectful and safe.

Eleanor Dzandza (7)
Brooke CE (VC) Primary School, Brooke

Jonty

J oyful Jonty is always happy
O tters are my favourite creature and guinea pigs
N ibbles and treats in their bowl make them squeal with delight
T hat is a nice pet
Y ou can be anything you want to be.

Jonty (7)
Brooke CE (VC) Primary School, Brooke

Toby B

T alented is for Toby and fun
O thers say I am very kind and helpful
B is for brilliant, that's what I am at skiing
Y oung but clever and courageous

B rave, beautiful and adventurous.

Toby Bellwood (7)
Brooke CE (VC) Primary School, Brooke

George

G is for great and mate
E is for energetic and magnetic
O is for original and individual
R is for ready and steady
G is for good and should
E xcited to read and learn.

George Bircham (8)
Brooke CE (VC) Primary School, Brooke

Cecily

C aring and sharing
E xcited and anxious
C ourageous and cheerful
I have a dog and a cat, I love them both
L ove myself all the time
Y oung and a cheerleader.

Cecily (7)
Brooke CE (VC) Primary School, Brooke

Katie

K atie is clever and joyful
A lways ready and super helpful
T alented, beautiful and adventurous
I nteresting, respectful and generous
E xcited, good, and likes books.

Katie Bellwood (7)
Brooke CE (VC) Primary School, Brooke

Imogen

I is for incredible
M is for mighty
O thers think I'm clever
G lamorous, bright and helpful
E xcellent and inventive
N aughty and sometimes brave.

Imogen Wright (7)
Brooke CE (VC) Primary School, Brooke

Kieran

K ing of the world
I like gaming
E very day I eat bananas
R oblox is my game to play
A pples help you to be healthy and I like them
N ice to my family.

Kieran Warman (7)
Brooke CE (VC) Primary School, Brooke

Zoey

Z oey is a lover of horses
O n the fields, you will find me
E very time the music plays, my dancing is ablaze
Y ou are you and I am me, so let's be the best we can be.

Zoey Holleman (8)
Brooke CE (VC) Primary School, Brooke

Toby S

T alented and terrific Toby
O ranges are my favourite fruit
B rave and behaved, I like to wear a suit with fruit
Y es I am

S porty, happy and active.

Toby Swietlik (8)
Brooke CE (VC) Primary School, Brooke

Jake

J ake Charles Wright is my full name
A ll the time I enjoy playing football
K itties are my pets, Daisy small and Bo big
E ngland is where I live, in Kirstead House.

Jake (7)
Brooke CE (VC) Primary School, Brooke

Felix

F elix, king of the playground
E legant, the best around
L ate at night I put on my cape
I fight crime around the world
X -ray vision to save everyone.

Felix Mott (7)
Brooke CE (VC) Primary School, Brooke

Audrey

A mazing and kind
U nique and unusual
D angerous and mischievous
R eady and respectful
E xcellent and exciting
Y oung and thoughtful.

Audrey Fairhurst (7)
Brooke CE (VC) Primary School, Brooke

Sergio

S uper Serg
E xcited to play
R iver is my dog
G reat today
I love football, Liverpool are the best
O n the field, you will find me.

Sergio Howard (7)
Brooke CE (VC) Primary School, Brooke

Harry

H appy Harry is nice
A nd football is fun to play
R eading is good
R eady to learn all the time
Y ou are amazing at running.

Harry Ashmole (7)
Brooke CE (VC) Primary School, Brooke

Isaac

I 'm as fast as a cheetah
S illy sometimes
A dventurous I am
A ctive when I play
C heese on toast is my favourite.

Isaac (8)
Brooke CE (VC) Primary School, Brooke

Israh The Greatest

My name is Israh the greatest
Well the greatest for me, I wake up in the morning and see
A tree blossoms to the best it can be
Just the same as me
As the clouds go grey
And it starts to rain
My little tree will grow today
As I stare into the cloudy night sky
I hug my pillow and say goodnight
Even if the tree won't bloom
I'll go and stare at the moon
I'm happy with the way I am
My name is Israh the greatest
For me and only me.

Israh Azgaou (8)
Falconbrook Primary School, Battersea

Lillys Are Gone

L ittle one
I mpossible is possible
L egible songs
L oving family
Y ou can be anything
S himmering stars

A mazing world
R abbits are very cute
E lephants are healthy and strong

G lorious thing
O range is a healthy fruit
N othing can be something
E ntering inside.

Asma Nishat (8)
Falconbrook Primary School, Battersea

It's Springtime

The grass grows high
The sun shines until the night
The flowers bloom and then birds sing
The rain clouds are ready to shine on the gorgeous plants
So let's celebrate spring.

Iman Asif (8)
Falconbrook Primary School, Battersea

Jiu-Jitsu

I train in jiu-jitsu
I defend myself against people
I try to work for a green belt.

Archie Martin (8)
Falconbrook Primary School, Battersea

This Is Me

I love to colour
It makes me happy
Some things make me sad
Like hurt and pain, people suffer from it
I hate when people get hurt
Once I look at it, it makes me feel upset
But most of the times I am happy
Here are some things that are super special
My teddy, I know I'm too big for one but
I never judge a book by its cover, so should you
Never say things to people
Also, you're never negative
I am kind
I don't like to wear hats but I have a cat
I love school trips but I hate when art rips.

Zara Holden (9)
Montgomery Primary Academy, Sparkbrook

This Is Me

This is me
I love the colour blue
My name is Zara
My favourite lessons are maths and reading
My hobby is art
My target is to reach my twelve times tables
I would like to benefit from literacy
My favourite book is the BFG
I am proud of who I am and I will always be
I love to read and learning is my hobby
I want to invest in my learning
But my teacher does enough.

Zara Naz Asif (9)
Montgomery Primary Academy, Sparkbrook

This Is Me

This is me,
I love butterflies,
I love my beautiful hair,
I love nature,
I love swimming,

I don't like bullies,
I don't like spending money,
I don't like nuts,

I like scribbling
I like being bold
I like learning
And my wish is to go to university.

Maria Jamil (9)
Montgomery Primary Academy, Sparkbrook

All About Me

This is me
My name is Issa
I love school, school is cool
I like to colour, I like to play
I love to come to school every day
I like to watch TV
Especially watching movies
I also like playing outside in the sun
Which is really fun
When I'm done
I go away from the sun.

Issa Abdulnahed (8)
Montgomery Primary Academy, Sparkbrook

This Is Me

This is me
What a person to be
Karolina is my name
Being a student is my game
My hair is as blonde as topaz
I am a Roblox fan
But hate beans in a can
I love learning and reading
Especially with someone good at teaching
My teacher is amazing, and always praising
She helps with my work
I struggle with it and she makes me smile
What a feeling to be.

Karolina Malon (9)
Moor Park Primary School, Bispham

This Is Me

T his is me
H ally, my friend, loves to have tea
I have the best teacher ever
S ienna in my class is so clever

I will love my mom forever
S easide is my favourite time, with family together

M y mommy loves the weather
E lla is my mom's friend, but she loves to be a good fella.

Louisa Lee (9)
Moor Park Primary School, Bispham

Me!

S ienna is my name
I love my cats
E smee is one of my besties
N aomi is my friend
N o one loves me as much as my family
A nd I love them back

M atilda and Mia are my other two besties
A re you getting bored?
Y ou're my friend too!

Sienna May Bampton (9)
Moor Park Primary School, Bispham

My Favourite Animal

Green and white with a hint of yellow
This little bird is a quacking fellow
Found in ponds and sometimes lakes
They can't fly but they can wait
Feed them bread and they'll be happy
I have named one Flappy
It's a duck if you couldn't guess
And in my opinion, they are the best.

Alfie Jai (9)
Moor Park Primary School, Bispham

This Is Me

T iny in size
H appy at heart
I love animals
S leep is what I do all day

I really love my family
S ometimes I like to do cooking

M y name is Esmee
E lephants are so cute, they have long trunks and their ears are so flappy.

Esmee Pogson (10)
Moor Park Primary School, Bispham

Milo And Bobby

Hi, my name is Milo
I can speak a bit of French
I have a dog called Bobby
He is a very loving doggy
He is as fluffy as a cloud
Also when he barks, he's very loud
He loves to play ball
When he jumps on me, he is tall
I also love football
This is me.

Milo Clarke (10)
Moor Park Primary School, Bispham

This Is Me

L ily is my name
I ndependent is what I am
L ying is not what I do
Y ellow is my second favourite colour

S miling is my game
U nsure of some things, but I persevere
E veryone I know is my friend and family.

Lily Sue (9)
Moor Park Primary School, Bispham

This Is Me

M y name is Mia
I love my pets
A nd I love food

C ats are the worst
A nd dogs are lovely
R uby is my sister
M angoes are the best
E ggs are my favourite
N ow is the end.

Mia Carmen (10)
Moor Park Primary School, Bispham

This Is Me

L acie is my name
A nd I like hot chocolate
C ake is my favourite
I love my family and friends
E veryone in my class is kind to me.

Lacie-Mae (9)
Moor Park Primary School, Bispham

The Mean Twin

I'm River and I have an evil twin
She's wretched and she likes to win
I get picked on, bullied and laughed at, while she has all the fun
She loves money like my greedy dad
While I sit on my bed and write
That smartypants always thinks she's right
What princess? I roll my eyes
I have hidden talents, I can sing
While her head is in the clouds
She's shallow while I'm in deep
We may be twins but we are so different
It's time to be upfront
Rachel and River make up Lucy
That's me!

Lucy Johnson (11)
Our Lady Queen Of Peace Catholic Engineering College, Skelmersdale

All About Me

I am so very quiet, but when it comes to ponies I'm really so bright.
My hobby is football but hobbies are horrible, I'm not good at it.
Sports are spectacular and I'm great at running in rugby
Also, I'm great at dodging in dodgeball.
My favourite animals are cats, rabbits and ponies.
Rabbits are runaway creatures, but they are cute, cuddly and soft.
You can do tricks with them like making them go up, down and turn around.
Ponies are perfect for being pretty, cheeky and fluffy
They love to frolic about, free in the field.
Cats are careful, they take care when they land everywhere
Some people are scared of cats because they can scratch.
Meowww
And that is all from me.

Tamara Al Jammal (9)
Pilling St John's CE School, Pilling

Me And My Perfect Pony

I am a girl who's merry and bright
When it comes to sweet ponies and horses
I own a handsome pony
Whose name is Max
We love to go on hacks
All around the tracks, long and short
We are keen and willing to try every time
But it's sad in winter
Because it gets dark too early
But, in spring and summer, it's light once more
So our joy is back
And the pony club we go to
We camp and do rallies
Which puts us in competitive moods
That's me and marvellous Max
I love him very much.

Aurora Wrigley (9)
Pilling St John's CE School, Pilling

To Make Me

Two bright blue eyes
Twenty-four pearly white teeth
A spoonful of intelligence
Add more or less, according to taste
Bags of laughter
A dash of defensive skill
Three teaspoons of kindness
A hint of fun
And a shelf-ful of books

Method
Add all of these together in a caring home
Mix with a little brother
Add lots of fresh air and exercise
Leave to grow for eleven years and one month
And you've made me!

Joseph Goth (11)
Pilling St John's CE School, Pilling

My Favourite Dog, Ocean

My favourite dog, Ocean
Helps me when I'm sad
She wipes away my tears
And that makes me glad
She's always there to greet me when I come through the door
She's very polite, my Ocean
If you tell her to sit, she will give you her paw
I wish she would live a lifetime
I don't know what I would do
She makes my life so special
My perfect Ocean blue.

Amelia Jayne Ratcliffe (7)
Pilling St John's CE School, Pilling

Wicked Wildlife

I do not have a short tail
I eat leaves
You cannot ride on me
I have spotty skin
I do not have feathers
I have black shoes
I have a black tongue
I have a bit of fear
I am slightly furry
I have antlers
I have long eyelashes
This is my favourite animal!
What is it?

Answer: A giraffe.

Elsie Ellis (9)
Pilling St John's CE School, Pilling

How To Make Maiyah Jayne

First, you need a tablespoon of smartness
Then you need half a teaspoon of braveness
After, put in a big bowl of craziness and another big bowl for happiness
Secondly, put in a teaspoon of beauty and a small bowl of emotion
Finally, add some funniness and bake for eight and a half years.

Maiyah Newbould (8)
Pilling St John's CE School, Pilling

How To Make Me

First, add half a spoon of sports
Secondly, add half a bottle of beauty
Then, add a full bottle of happiness with a splash of animals
Then, add a third of brave
Then, finally, add a pinch of compassion
Bake for eight and a half years.

Eliza Clitheroe (8)
Pilling St John's CE School, Pilling

This Is My Bestie

A kennings poem

An actor actress
A best bestie
A helpful helper
A prancer dancer
A smiley smiler
A giggly giggler
A kind kicker
A popular pop
This is my bestie, Abbey
And she is like a sister to me.

Ruby Sarson (10)
Pilling St John's CE School, Pilling

Football

Football is an incredibly good game
Everybody is cool
England didn't train in the Euros
They were just swimming in the pool

My least favourite team is Aston Villa
It's bad, like my incredibly mad dad
He plays like a child that plays for Longniddry Villa

Lots of footballers play in the rain
Lots of players play when they are in pain
Don't be aggressive, like that player, Dan
Dan earned himself a lifetime ban

Football is incredible.

Harry Burgoyne (9)
Preston Tower Primary School, Prestonpans

All About Me

T ime flies by as I grow taller and taller
H appy like the big, bright, fiery sun
I nterested in trying new and wonderful things
S mart, got the brains like a cheeky monkey

I may be small but I am an incredibly fast little runner
S trong, like a magical reindeer

M adly crazy when my pals are around
E asy going like a curious puppy on the sidewalk.

Ashley Tait (9)
Preston Tower Primary School, Prestonpans

This Is Me

T oday, I played my Xbox
H ello Dylan, my brother runs in and turns it off
I don't talk to him for the rest of the day
S ay something, he yells and I turn away

I n basketball lessons I don't miss a shot
S hould I get a move up

M y mum tells me I should talk to my brother again
E xcept, I don't.

Dylan Gare (9)
Preston Tower Primary School, Prestonpans

This Is Me

T he people in my family are really kind
H ibs are my favourite football team by a mile
I am as quick as lightning, charging down to the ground
S ummer is my favourite season

I love playing with my friends
S oon, I will be a pro football player

M onkeys are my favourite animals
E ight is my lucky number.

Josh Quinn (9)
Preston Tower Primary School, Prestonpans

This Is Me

I love my dog
His name is Ziggy
He will always be my buddy
He goes for a shower when he is muddy
I always feed him
He is so fluffy
I take him on a walk every Saturday and Sunday
He gets an extra biscuit on Monday
He has been in a training test
He will always be a pest
But he is the best
This is what makes him, well, him
This is me.

Aaron Trendell (9)
Preston Tower Primary School, Prestonpans

This Is Me

T igers are fast and fearless, like me
H appiness is the key to my heart
I am an ice cube on a cold day, but when it's sunny, that ice cube breaks
S assiest girl

I am as grateful as a monkey
S ummer is the best season

M y best friend is as crazy as a kangaroo
E ggs are the best.

Lois Buchannan (9)
Preston Tower Primary School, Prestonpans

This Is Me

T he 25th of November is my birthday
H appy with my besties
I like to read
S ummer is my favourite season

I ce cream, my favourite flavour is vanilla
S unny days are wonderful with ice cream

M y pet is called Oreo and I love her so much
E very day I love her even more.

Ava Gray (9)
Preston Tower Primary School, Prestonpans

This Is Me

I love to read, my favourite book is Horrid Henry
When I read it makes me happy

I love dogs, because they are kind
Dogs make me happy

My favourite food is pizza
Eating it makes me happy

I love to ride my bike in summer
Cycling makes me happy

My friends are Erin and Aimee
They make me happy.

Skye Mcewan (9)
Preston Tower Primary School, Prestonpans

My Curious, Friendly Frenchie, Robbie

My Frenchie, Robbie
Curious, friendly
Nosey, cute, crazy and fun
Loves to give a sniff at everything
Is an amazing TikTok dancer
Loves yummy treats
Also loves going on walks, especially with me
Happy all the time
He is quite small by the way
His rope toy is his favourite
But most of all, he loves playing with me!

Olivia Linda Thorburn
Preston Tower Primary School, Prestonpans

This Is Me

R oblox is my game, it is my very favourite
O nly Roblox has any game you want to play
B eing nice to people and letting them have a go
L ove is a nice thing to celebrate on a birthday
O n my birthday, I hope for roller skates
X box is a good console, and on it I can play Roblox.

Kayla Reid (9)
Preston Tower Primary School, Prestonpans

This Is Me

Climbing is something I like to do
It makes me feel alive
Like I am the only person in the world
As I get higher, my grip tightens
Praying the ropes will hold
And then
I am at the top
Now, I lean back and start my descent
And in time for the next wall
Because I am a climber of the life ladder.

Harry Davidson (10)
Preston Tower Primary School, Prestonpans

This Is Me

I like Christmas and I like to read books
I am so happy like a puppy playing in the hot sun
I am bright like a happy rainbow in the hot sun
I love dogs, cats and rabbits
My family is cool like me
Be yourself
Do what makes you happy
Be happy like me, enjoying pizza and cool ice cream in the hot sun.

Lucy Betts (9)
Preston Tower Primary School, Prestonpans

Christmas

C hristmas is the best time of the year
H appiness fills the room
R iley is my name
I am very smart
S weets are the best food
T oys are my favourite
M y mum is the best
A re you good or bad?
S weets are the best food.

Riley Harrison (9)
Preston Tower Primary School, Prestonpans

This Is Me
A Kennings poem

I am
As fast as a car
Fast like Sonic
Sometimes angry, like Anger from Inside Out
Really awesome
Friendly, like a nice kid
Fun as ever
Silly as a clown
Curious like a puppy
Smart like Melvin from Captain Underpants
A fast book reader
This is me!

Callum Stewart (9)
Preston Tower Primary School, Prestonpans

My Favourite Animal

It's a sea animal
Can't live on land and cannot fly
Normally swims with others
Kind
Makes a weird noise
Flips and dives in the sea
Has a fin and is grey
Eats fish
Has blue eyes and is cute
What is it?

Answer: A dolphin.

Ava Rawlison (9)
Preston Tower Primary School, Prestonpans

This Is Me

R obyn is my amazing sister
O nly no spicy things for me
B eing nice to everyone is important
L ove everyone in my family, though my dad is the best
O n Sundays, I eat homemade pancakes
X is the last letter in my name.

Alex Kubis-Simpson (9)
Preston Tower Primary School, Prestonpans

This Is Me

Energetic I am
People call me crazy
Even though I'm a sleepy person
Sometimes, but I'm a super
Kind, funny, fun and artistic person
That's okay because I'm staying this way
Because it's who I am
And it's me.

Sophie Dickson (9)
Preston Tower Primary School, Prestonpans

This Is Me

I'm fast like a dog
I'm helpful like a helper
I'm as sweet as candy
I love dogs, as cute as peaches
And hamsters
And guinea pigs
And fish
I'm as happy as a unicorn
My eyes are blue
This is me.

Georgie Ritchie (9)
Preston Tower Primary School, Prestonpans

This Is Me

S uper fast, like lightning
O n my way to be the best
P art of a family and a group
H appier than ever and always doing something
I always try my hardest
E nergetic like all my friends.

Sophie Scott (9)
Preston Tower Primary School, Prestonpans

This Is Me
A kennings poem

I am a
Big Starbucks fan
Horse lover
Summer whisperer
Roblox player
Big fan of white and blue
Fresh fruit eater
Cat owner
Kind and happy person
Bay and grey rider
And that's what makes me, me!

Lucy Spence (9)
Preston Tower Primary School, Prestonpans

Who I Am

What I like is drawing people
How do I do it? I draw them bold
Oh, how good they are

I love technology, I can't resist it
A computer, I write poems with it
My life is the best and I am who I am.

Logan Brand (9)
Preston Tower Primary School, Prestonpans

This Is Me

T houghtful
H appy
I ce is cold
S illy is me

I ntelligent
S ensible

M y dream is to be a kind, helpful vet
E xcited like a hamster.

Emillie Clark (9)
Preston Tower Primary School, Prestonpans

My Football Team

My team is Longniddry
I have matches every Sunday
I am a winger
I like whizzing up the wing
It is my dream to play for Tottenham
But I think that even if I play all day
It will never happen, anyway.

Harry Fitzpatrick (9)
Preston Tower Primary School, Prestonpans

Karting

I love go-karting
Sometimes it's tough
I crash once or twice
But I get back in and win
I start another race
Bang
Their karts crash into the wall
Again, I win.

Ollie Gray (9)
Preston Tower Primary School, Prestonpans

This Is Me

I feel all warm and tingly inside
I feel like a bubble about to burst
I feel like I have butterflies in my stomach
What am I?

Answer: Happiness.

Jessica Skinner (9)
Preston Tower Primary School, Prestonpans

This Is Me

F ree as a fly
R ight as a smart kid
E xcited
D ynamite
D oes great
I love my mum
E xercise!

Freddie Young
Preston Tower Primary School, Prestonpans

Changing Over Time

Throughout the years, we change our mind
For example, I'll show you mine

I used to love the colour blue
But now I like the colour pink too

Playing with my small cousin was a great joy
But now I just want to play with my toy

When I was two, I started wearing glasses
To help me through life and classes
My teacher now gives me more passes

As I got things right
I felt very bright
I now concentrate on my work a lot more
If you would like, I could give you a tour

Growing up, I was interested in rabbits
But now that I'm older, I have many other habits

Now that I'm nine
I'm sure I am totally fine
But knowing me

I can see
As my mind fully clears
I'll surely change over the years.

Muskaan Ahmed (9)
Sacred Heart RC Primary School, Blackburn

Character Strengths Make My Personality

S miling is the secret of my happiness
E motions teach me self-regulation
L ove of learning helps me design awesome Lego architecture
F riendship is as precious as a jewel for me

R oaring storms can't stop me from exploring extreme weather
E xploding like a volcano is not my nature
G ratitude is the key of spreading kindness and love
U nity makes me very strong
L eadership helps me motivate others
A ppreciation of beauty helps me to notice people skills
T eamwork makes the dream work
I conic people inspire me
O bey people so they can obey you back
N obility makes me a really humble person.

Ipsit Jagtap (7)
Sherington Primary School, London

Me

This is me
This is me, trying to leave my mark on the surface of the Earth
Striving to become a role model for girls just like me
This is me
Living my life my way
Looking to the future, not the past
Just being me
This is me with no apologies and no regrets
This is me
Living life to the fullest
Enjoying every moment and cherishing the things and people I care about
Me hoping to find my way through the fog
And finally setting eyes on my dreams
This is me
Proud, bold, phenomenal me.

Glory Ano Sunday (10)
South Rise Primary School, London

The Key To Me!

Loyalty
Power
Kindness
And empathy
Hi I'm Krista, this is me

Bravery
Courage
Honesty
And more
Are the key to my personality

Race
Gender
Culture and religion
Are some things I respect

Mushrooms
Grapefruit
And BBQ sauce
Are things I neglect

Loyalty
Power
Kindness
And empathy
This is the key to me.

Krista Thapa (9)
South Rise Primary School, London

A Recipe For Rebecca

You will need:

One tablespoon of positivity
Three shakes of energetic fun
Two teaspoons of responsibility
A sprinkle of kindness and love
500g of crazy personality
Three pinches of sugar and jokes
200g of creativity

And lastly, a bowl full of me!

Rebecca Roper (10)
South Rise Primary School, London

Be You, No Matter What Anybody Says

Be you
Be yourself, no matter what happens
Be you
The skies are blue
The clouds are white
They are one
Be like them
Be one
The wind blows smoothly
The water flows
Together they say be you
Let's all live together
So we can bring peace.

Desireoluwa Oduneye (10)
South Rise Primary School, London

Late Night Stories

Sitting in bed with a light shining down on me
A book in my hands, the words mixing together
One line shifting into another
Ding
The clock strikes midnight, signalling me I should go to sleep
The light dims down into darkness
Each word fades away as the minutes pass
Sleep
Images forming in my mind, creating a blurry vision
My eyes fluttering shut and a yawn escaping my lips
00:02
Every inch of my body and brain is telling me to sleep
But what about the words that follow
Or the kingdoms to visit
Maybe I'll get to go on a new adventure tomorrow.

Maisie Wilkinson (13)
Spen Valley Sports College, Liversedge

How To Make Leah

Mix in some sugar, add in some spice
Squeeze in some honey
That'll make me sweet and nice

Now, let's go outside, lace up my boots
Just give me a ball
And then I'll shoot

Let's get inside and get cosy,
Get on my fluffy socks
Time to chill out
And let's play some Roblox!

Leah Womersley (11)
Spen Valley Sports College, Liversedge

Christmas Fun All Around

M y family all together
I t is all around with joy
A ll my friends here with me
H aving fun

T oday is a great day
A ll around the fire
Y ou and I all snug
L ove all around
O h Santa, are you watching us?
R osie the Christmas star.

Miah Taylor (11)
Spen Valley Sports College, Liversedge

I Am Sarim

My favourite thing about me is I like to draw
The ingredients that make me are
I like talking about elephants because they are huge
My dream for the future is to be Captain Sperm Whale
When I am sad I like to stay alone and sing songs.

Sarim Khan (10)
Springhallow School, Ealing

KJ Studios

My favourite thing
Being happy
Helping others to not be bullied
My dream is making TikTok videos for myself
I feel better when I draw.

Kj Johnson (10)
Springhallow School, Ealing

This Is Me

O nly I know all of my favourite things and now I will share
L asagne
U nity with people, like a gathering or a meetup
W atching TV, my favourite TV shows are Steven Universe and Victorious
A ssisting other people, I like to be of use
S aying drip, stupid, naruto and UvU
E nrolling in activities where I meet new people
Y es, now I can tell you what I hate and what will make me angry or sad
I gnoring me, you don't want to do that

F ighting and the only time I am doing that is when I am playfighting
U sing other people's things, if it's theirs, it is mine
N ever saying yes, my parents do this
M y PC, phone, TV, my mom, dad, everyone in my family
F riends, everything I've seen so for in the wonderful life
A nd last but not least, to be myself.

Seyi Fowowe (10)
St John Fisher Primary School, Littlemore

Pick Me, Teacher

Pick me, pick me
My hand is up high
Teacher won't pick me
Why, why, why?

Then, the teacher picks me
My face has gone red
Because the thing I was going to say
Has gone out of my head.

Tyreign Thomas (10)
St John Fisher Primary School, Littlemore

What Emotion Am I?

You sit up and your vision is blurry
You rub your eyes and look around
It's all dark
You begin to shiver, feel unsafe and lonely
Nobody is around to help
You try to speak but no matter how hard you try
You just cannot
You frantically look all around
But no sight of light is anywhere
Eyes start to stare and harass you
You close yours, hoping it's all a dream
But it isn't
They are trying to manipulate you
Or at least that was what it felt like anyways
A tear trickles down your cheek
You feel powerless
Which emotion am I?

Emily Mcmahon (9)
Westlea Primary School, Westlea

This Is Me

This is me
My eyes are as big and brown as a chocolate bar
To help me see wonderful people
This is me, my ears are as long as a rabbit's ear
To help me hear
Lovely comments about me and other people
This is me, my nose is as clever as a scientist to help me smell my dad and mum
So, when I cuddle them, like a soft warm panda, whatever happens, we never forget about each other
This is me
My mouth is flexible and bright as a banana
So I could smile at everyone I see
Even if they're strangers
This is me
When I'm out with my family, happiness spreads out
Even In the gloomy dark space that describes my powerful feelings
This is me

When I'm upset, the only thing that makes me feel happier
Is my one and only family and friends
This is me.

Yusuf Karakaya (11)
Westlea Primary School, Westlea

This Is Me

Anger, boiling and bubbling
Ready to tip over the edge
A volcano of emotion, a crescendo
Drowning out the fear, yet fuelling the sadness
A never-ending battle, a ceaseless fight, endless

Fear, creeping up the walls
Whispering shadows, paralysing thoughts
What if
It all goes wrong, what if
I fail, what if

Sadness, a constant rainy day
Gradually piling up, forming puddles in the path
They swish, they splash
It builds up like ash
And covers almost all

Happiness, a fairground ride
Smiles, laughs and life
An overpowering feeling of energy
A calming stroll through the park

A balance between emotions
A tightrope walk, a scale
Of which can keep you feeling great.

Otter Ley (10)
Westlea Primary School, Westlea

Me

Sometimes, I feel like I can fly high to the sky,
Away from today and into tomorrow.
Sometimes, I feel like I'm glowing and flowing,
Blowing and knowing and having fun.
Sometimes, I feel like I'm going to burst and do the worst today.
Sometimes, at night, I feel all tight, just like I'm going to bite.
Sometimes, at night, I think of the light just sinking away from me.
Sometimes, at night, it feels just right, just like it's all for me.
Sometimes, I feel sad, sometimes, I feel mad.
Sometimes, I feel brave,
And sometimes, I feel saved.

Emily M (10)
Westlea Primary School, Westlea

All About Me

A ll of me is special
L iving with my family is great
L earning with friends who are great is epic

A ll of my family are precious to me, like a gem
B rothers are the only siblings I have, but I don't care
O ut of my favourite things, it would be my family
U nder my skin is feelings
T hey make me who I am

M yself is so special
E very last bit, even if one brother is gone, he will still be in my heart.

Iris Hinder (9)
Westlea Primary School, Westlea

Newcastle United

N ever give in,
E lectric is in our souls.
W e will
C onquer anything and everything.
A lways have faith and stay strong.
S ituations will come, but we will always succeed.
T ake every game and opportunity solidly,
L ive to the end.
E ndurance is key, not just a winning spree.

U nited together we stand.
T ogether, everything is just a little thing.
D ie together, live together.

Jaxon Coe (9)
Westlea Primary School, Westlea

It's Me

O ne boy who loves history and keeps it alive
L ikes football and cricket
L ikes World War Two a lot
I wear army gear everywhere
E ven when I'm at home, I keep it alive

L ikes it all, wants to join the army
I nteresting I am, he is very daring
B ecause his family was there in World War Two
B ut will he change his mind
Y ou never know.

Oliver Libby (9)
Westlea Primary School, Westlea

This Is Me

T he sun shines and I like it
H ow are dogs so cute?
E verything I will sing to
A nd my favourite colour is purple

S mall things I like
M y mum is kind and my dad
O ne is the best number
L ong things I don't like
A nd cats I like
R eading I like
E very day I am happy
K ind and nice.

Thea Smolarek (9)
Westlea Primary School, Westlea

Anger

Anger is like a mirror
Reflecting the things that make you heartbroken
An enraged replica that bursts in with no warning
It controls you like a puppet, forcing you to kick, swear and punch
All other emotions cower in fear, they hide and pray for their lives
Once the anger is gone back into the deepest part of your body, waiting for its next outburst
The other emotions come out of hiding.

Rizwaan (11)
Westlea Primary School, Westlea

Gaming Rules

G ammon tastes nice
A nteaters look cool
M ilk tastes lovely but can go rotten
I ce tastes lovely
N achos with cheese rules
G orillas are smelly

R oots look like trees
U nder the sea is a good song
L eft is my favourite direction
E arth is where I live
S windon is the best.

Toby Sieluzycki (9)
Westlea Primary School, Westlea

All About Me

L ove
E xciting
O striches are huge to me

D ogs are fluffy
E nergetic
N ever judge
N ever hurt others
I 'm kind
S mall

H edgehogs are cute
E lephants are ginormous
D umb
G ullible
E ggs are smelly
S hy.

Leo Hedges (10)
Westlea Primary School, Westlea

This Is Me

I ncredible is what I am

A mazing is what I am
M agnificent is what I am

S mart is what I am
P ersevering is what I am
E nchanting is what I am
C ourageous is what I am
I nspiring is what I am
A dventurous is what I am
L uxurious is what I am.

Bailey Mussard (10)
Westlea Primary School, Westlea

This Is Me

I'm nine and a half
So this is going to have that many lines
I'm helpful and smart, I like ice tea and Costa
My favourite food is chicken nuggets from McDonald's and pizza
I love dogs but I can't have one because my dad is allergic
I have a family of four
My dad, mum and brother
I like to listen to music.

Samantha Belina
Westlea Primary School, Westlea

Who Am I?

My short wavy hair is dark brown
My eyes are glimmering brown with a hint of green
My glasses are rounded blue and black, like the moon
I am a relaxed, fearless person

My favourite colour is mint green and blue
My dream place is NYC
I like to go rollerskating
Who am I?

Answer: Jess.

Jessica (11)
Westlea Primary School, Westlea

Gaming Is The Best

G aming is great
A wsome sports
M agic
I ce cream
N ice parents
G reat food

I ndependence
S iena

T akeaways
H ilarious jokes
E ggs

B irthday
E aster
S pace
T oys.

Jenson Cain (10)
Westlea Primary School, Westlea

This Is Me

F unny conversations
A lot of memories
M any holidays
I mmy is the best cousin
L ove
Y ou would be jealous

B elle is my nickname
E nergetic
L aughter
L ayla, Isla and Elissia are my best friends
E verlasting phonecalls.

Isabelle Le Leivre (10)
Westlea Primary School, Westlea

Mental Health

M y dog is cute
E ating ice cream is fun
N othing is impossible
T ell a teacher
A mazing dogs
L ove blue

H ate tomatoes
E verything is amazing
A pples are healthy
L oving cats
T remendous cake
H appy hair.

Amelia Cheesley (10)
Westlea Primary School, Westlea

This Is Me

    E verything about me is unique
    L ovely me
    L ong days playing with my friends
    I 'm different in my own unique way
    E veryone is beautiful just the way they are

I have red hair, hazel eyes, freckles, earrings, wavy hair
And I am eleven years old
Who am I?

Ellie Mortimer (11)
Westlea Primary School, Westlea

Cookies

C ole is cool
O pen up the chocolate wrapper
O ut in the jungle, gorillas roam
K rakens are mythical creatures
I love cookies so much
E at cookies every second
S wans are horrible, beastly, ugly and scary creatures. One sank its teeth into my finger.

Cole Farley (9)
Westlea Primary School, Westlea

Who Am I?

I have dark brown, straight hair
My eyes are light blue
My favourite colours are teal and purple
I love eating food, especially lasagne

I have a cat called Ollie
I like listening to music
My favourite film is Encanto
My dream job is an actor or an author.

Aislinn Thompson (11)
Westlea Primary School, Westlea

This Is Me

My heart traps all the good things and buries them in the dark
Where a loud roar couldn't destroy its inspiration
My lungs explode with excitement like a firework when I see my hobbies
I am so lucky to have a life like this
Every little bit of me I wouldn't sell.

Nikola Kozlowska (10)
Westlea Primary School, Westlea

This Is Me

I am as clumsy as a birthday clown
This is me
I dream to become
A basketball player
This is me
I wonder if I will become really successful
I hope I will become a famous basketball player
This is me
I am as strong as a massive tiger
This is me.

Janelle (10)
Westlea Primary School, Westlea

Football

F ootball is the best
O utside, I like to play football
O utside in the field is our club
T eam game
B alls are the best to kick
A ll my family like football
L ots of footballs
L ots of kids like football.

Jackson Bridgman (9)
Westlea Primary School, Westlea

This Is Me

O llie
L ovely natured
L ove Spurs
I ntelligent
E xcellent at football

W allis
A nice person
L ikes to help people
L ikes to be helpful
I deal friend
S uper kind.

Ollie Wallis (11)
Westlea Primary School, Westlea

Isabelle

I ntelligent me
S ometimes, I can't wait for tomorrow
A wesome me
B ed is my safe place where I relax
E xcited me
L ong walks outside with my friends
L ovely me
E veryone is awesome the way they are.

Isabelle Fraser (11)
Westlea Primary School, Westlea

This Is Me

This is me.
I am as quick as a cheetah.
This is me.
I dream of being a surgeon.
This is me.

I hope I get good grades.
This is me.
I wonder if I am strong or weak.
This is me.

I am brave as a tiger.
This is me.

Josh Saji (10)
Westlea Primary School, Westlea

This Is Me

L egendary
I am funny
V ery kind
E ndless amounts of energy
R eally loving
P articularly patient
O ften playing on my Xbox
O nly boy in the house
L ike a mirror of my father.

Kieran Butler (10)
Westlea Primary School, Westlea

Birthday

B est day of the year
I nteresting
R eal cake, chocolate cake
T he presents, and family time
H appy and joyful
D ecorations and food
A mazingness and joy
Y es, it is the best day ever.

Izzy Harper (10)
Westlea Primary School, Westlea

Chicken

C hicken is good hot
H orrible chicken is raw
I cy chicken is not good
C hicken is good when it's seasoned
K ept nice chicken is good
E ating chicken is the best
N ever eat chicken bones.

Jermain Dube (10)
Westlea Primary School, Westlea

This Is Me

T ikTok dancing
H istory at school
I mogen Green
S wimming like a mermaid

I nto lots of sports
S loths and Thor

M cDonald's and curry
E d Sheeran on my phone.

Imogen Green (10)
Westlea Primary School, Westlea

This Is Me

Gaming and reading
Playing Five Nights At Freddy's
Playing some football

Doing my homework
Eating KFC
Having a party bucket

Helping my mother
And watching TV
Listening to some good songs.

Sayam (10)
Westlea Primary School, Westlea

This Is Me

J am is nice
A corns are hard
M ice are nice
E ggs are messy
S and is rock

B ells are loud
E ggs are smelly
L akes are deep
L akes are yuck.

James Bell (10)
Westlea Primary School, Westlea

Emily

E xciting as getting a new toy
M agnificent as a graceful and pink flamingo
I nteresting as a newborn baby
L oving as a new puppy
Y ourself, be yourself, do not change who you are.

Emily Pentecost (10)
Westlea Primary School, Westlea

This Is Me

T rouble
H ero
I nspired
S hort

I n bed all the time
S ausage fingers

M ilo listens, unlike Saidy and Dollie
E xcellent.

Ruby Burns (10)
Westlea Primary School, Westlea

Birthday

B rilliant
I love it
R emember to give me those presents
T he best day of the year
H appy times
D elicious cake
A lot of gifts
Y ay!

Sebastian Piechowicz (9)
Westlea Primary School, Westlea

Football

F ootball is the best
O utside of
O ur club
T he squad is excellent
B ig footballs
A re the top
L ots of training
L ots of matches.

Max Bunney (10)
Westlea Primary School, Westlea

This Is Me

This is me
I am as thin as a stick
This is me
I dream of nightmares
I hope I am brilliant
This is me
I wonder myself
This is me
I am as small as a mouse
This is me.

Arish Siddique (10)
Westlea Primary School, Westlea

What Emotion Am I?

I am known for my fury
My explosive rage
I have a never-ending temper
It can take over suddenly
Unless you are careful
What emotion am I?

Answer: Anger.

Morgan Salmon (9)
Westlea Primary School, Westlea

What Emotion Am I?

I'm watchful and wary of all things around
Looking up and down and all around at the ground
Staring at the wall, I'm listening around
If I'm scared, I won't be found.

Leo Jones (10)
Westlea Primary School, Westlea

What Am I?

I'm big when young
I'm small when old
I can't breathe but you can blow me out
I don't have lungs
What am I?

Answer: A candle.

Eliza Etmanska (10)
Westlea Primary School, Westlea

Birthday

B uilding memories
I ncredible
R eally cool
T o have fun
H appy
D elicious cake
A mazing
Y oung.

Maisie Bowles (10)
Westlea Primary School, Westlea

Maysie

M y life is awesome
A ll my family and friends are the best
Y ou are you
S uper
I like watching Encanto
E xcellent.

Maysie Cope (10)
Westlea Primary School, Westlea

Alfie

A mazing at life
L oves to watch anime
F antastic at netball
I ndecisive about ice cream
E specially better than other people.

Alfie Lusty (11)
Westlea Primary School, Westlea

This Is Me

C allum is amazing and awesome.
A m I arty?
L ike gaming and football.
L ove my family.
U nusual.
M ake magic.

Callum Shurey (10)
Westlea Primary School, Westlea

Happy

H elpful I can be
A mazing at art
P erfect I am
P eaceful is what I am
Y es, I am happy.

Billii-Mae Hemmings-Willott (11)
Westlea Primary School, Westlea

How To Make Me

I love honey
Animals make me happy
Movies rule
I like games
Animals are the best
I'm a very happy monster.

Rhys Huff (10)
Westlea Primary School, Westlea

What Emotion Am I?

I'm sprinting around
All over the place
My heart is pounding
And I'm not getting tired
What is my emotion?

Archie Walsh (10)
Westlea Primary School, Westlea

This Is Me

I am kind
A nd a good friend
N ever disrespectful
I am funny
S o, this is me.

Ianis Butnariu (10)
Westlea Primary School, Westlea

This Is Me

S o awesome
I love my family
L oving
L ove everyone
Y ou're amazing.

Jamie Lea (10)
Westlea Primary School, Westlea

This Is Me

My name is Noah
A very sporty boy
I am always on the move
Just like a robot toy
My favourite sport is cricket
I like football too
Golf is fantastic
There are so many sports I do
As you can see
My life is sport
It's really fun
Playing at the basketball court
I love to eat food
I love all Italian
Especially when pasta is cooked by my dad
Who, to me, is a very special man
I love my family
I have one brother
Mum and dad
At least they're no bother
I love making Lego

Technic is a challenge
Lego City is my favourite
Harry Potter, I can manage
The wilderness is the best
Climbing up the trees
Setting up tents
Avoiding the bees
I like to cook
Steaming spaghetti
Grating the cheese
Although the kitchen gets messy
I had Dave the dog
And Rosy the cat
Rosy was a sweetheart
Never chased a rat
Now you have read
All about me
This is my life
The life of Noah D.

Noah D (11)
Wood Lane Primary School, Bignall End

YOUNG WRITERS INFORMATION

We hope you have enjoyed reading this book – and that you will continue to in the coming years.

If you're the parent or family member of an enthusiastic poet or story writer, do visit our website **www.youngwriters.co.uk/subscribe** and sign up to receive news, competitions, writing challenges and tips, activities and much, much more! There's lots to keep budding writers motivated!

If you would like to order further copies of this book, or any of our other titles, then please give us a call or order via your online account.

Young Writers
Remus House
Coltsfoot Drive
Peterborough
PE2 9BF
(01733) 890066
info@youngwriters.co.uk

Join in the conversation!
Tips, news, giveaways and much more!

 YoungWritersUK  YoungWritersCW  youngwriterscw